I0711770

Guiding Principles for FFA Career Development Events (CDEs) and Leadership Development Events (LDEs)

Charles W. Byers, Ph.D.
Professor Emeritus
Agricultural Education
University of Kentucky
cwbyers1@windstream.net
859-492-2335

National Association of Agricultural Educators
One Paragon Centre
2525 Harrodsburg Road, Suite 200
Lexington, Kentucky 40504-3358
859-967-2892
www.NAAE.org

Table of Contents

Foreword

Wm. Jay Jackman, Ph.D., CAE
Executive Director (1996-2020)
National Association of Agricultural Educators
Lexington, Kentucky

For nearly 25 years I have had the privilege and joy of being the executive director of the National Association of Agricultural Educators (NAAE). During this time, I have received countless communiques from agricultural educators from all across the United States asking me to provide them a comment or a document they can use with their administrators to show that FFA is an integral component of their agricultural education program. My response to these inquiries usually was, "Well, is it?" It's a serious question. For you see if we truly believe in the agricultural education model (quality instruction in classrooms and laboratories, experiential learning, and leadership development) … and I do … then this model is not only *appropriate for every student* but it should be *delivered to every student*. If experiential learning, through supervised agricultural experiences (SAE), is a valuable part of the ag ed model, then it should be delivered to every student, not just a select few. If leadership education, through FFA, is a valuable part of the ag ed model, then it should be delivered to every student, not just a select few.

I learned this simple, yet remarkable, concept from my teacher, Dr. Charles W. Byers, in teaching methods classes at the University of Kentucky in the fall of 1984. I should say I learned this *formally* from Dr. Byers in the fall of 1984. Truth be told, even though I didn't realize it at the time, I was exposed to this simple, yet remarkable, concept from my own agriculture teachers when I was a student at Barren County High School in Glasgow, Kentucky. As a high school agriculture student, I didn't have an option to participate in only some parts of the ag ed model. My agriculture teachers expected me to participate in class, have a SAE and keep records on it, and be involved in FFA. I didn't have an option to pick and choose from these three components of the ag ed model.

So, to teachers who struggle to convince their administrators that FFA is an integral component of agricultural education, I say, "Well, is it? Is it truly integral in your local program for every student, not just a select few?" It must be if we truly believe in the ag ed model.

During Dr. Byers' exceptional career as a teacher educator, he taught hundreds of pre-service and in-service agriculture teachers that one way to make FFA an integral part of agricultural education for every student is through *local* career development events (CDEs) and leadership development events (LDEs). Following the instructional units we teach, with few exceptions, comes student assessment; we need to know if our students are learning well (and if they are not, it may be because we are not teaching well, but we'll save that discussion for another day). What could possibly be a better way to assess student learning than using a test of performance-based measures? Tests of performance-based measures for our students in our own agriculture classes are *local* CDEs and LDEs! Test or contest? In both, we are measuring student learning.

Dr. Byers didn't stop at teaching us that CDEs and LDEs can serve as our student assessments. He also taught us that the local FFA CDE and LDE can help motivate students to do their best. And, he went further to teach us how to apply to our teaching his 17 principles for using FFA CDEs and LDEs to motivate and enhance student learning. Even in our modern age of technology and social media, the rudimentary concepts presented in these 17 principles are as important and meaningful today as they were when Mr. Byers, an early-career agriculture teacher at Lowes High School in west Kentucky, motivated and taught Junior and others who won the state livestock judging contest many decades ago.

Whether you are a pre-service agricultural education student at a university, an early career agriculture teacher, or a seasoned agricultural educator, I challenge you to consider how you can apply these 17 principles in your teaching. I believe you will experience positive results in your teaching. I believe your students will be motivated to participate and to learn. I believe your administrators will no longer question how FFA is integral to your instructional program … because it will be!

Incidentally and personally, when I was a student and early in my career, Dr. Charles W. Byers was my professor, graduate assistantship supervisor, and my mentor. As my career progressed and now as it begins to wind down, Dr. Byers continues to be my mentor, my friend, and most importantly, my teacher. I cannot think of a higher accolade than to say of him, "He is my teacher!"

Commentary

Jeff Hayes
Teacher of Agriculture, Retired
Rockcastle County High School
Mt. Vernon, Kentucky

The 17 principles discussed in this publication provide a logical, fair and effective means for committed teachers to provide high quality instruction for all students. These 17 principles will prove invaluable to any teacher who can understand that the key purpose of the CDE/LDE is to enhance instruction, not just to win. I have used Dr. Byers' teachings throughout my twenty-seven years as an agriculture teacher and FFA advisor. I have a difficult time understanding why anyone would not implement his common-sense approach to instruction. In fact, I believe this publication should be required reading for anyone associated with education, especially those that work with student organizations. By implementing these principles, you can expect an increase in student motivation and enhanced student learning. Success in CDEs/LDEs is sure to follow.

Commentary

Matt Chaliff
Executive Secretary
Kentucky FFA Association
Frankfort, Kentucky

The best class I ever had in college was the graduate level Student Organizations class taught by Dr. Charles Byers. In spite of the fact that I faced a 90-minute drive home after class, I always wanted Dr. Byers to keep teaching! As a brand-new teacher, I found that not only were the stories about his time in the classroom entertaining, but that <u>Dr. Byers' principles worked in my classroom</u>. I know these 17 principles work because I have seen the results all over the Commonwealth of Kentucky.

I've met Junior! I've seen his national gold medal! I know that it is one of his most prized possessions nearly 50 years after he won it! (Refer to Principle 8!)

I believe with all my heart, if every teacher of agriculture in America would read this book and implement these strategies, we would see a world of difference. Our students would be more motivated, more students would be involved in our FFA chapters, teachers would have to spend less time practicing after school, and the list goes on. But most importantly, we would see a phenomenal increase in student learning … and hundreds -- maybe thousands -- of Junior's proudly displaying the records of their accomplishments for years to come!

Introduction

Over the years, I have asked numerous agriculture teachers how successful their agriculture program may be. Often, I got an answer sharing their students' success in the FFA such as the number of State or American Degrees received, number of state officers, number of state or national winners in CDEs/LDEs and proficiencies. These things are certainly good, but do not always tell the whole story. It would be helpful to have information on how these achievements were accomplished. Some criteria that may be just as important are as follows:

- How much each student enrolled in the program learned skills that helped them to succeed in the agriculture field, college, or the world of work.
- How students were prepared for life.

It would be nice to know that a high percentage of agriculture students after graduating would report that being an agriculture student and FFA member impacted their life in a meaningful and positive way.

The agriculture classroom should be a place where learning takes place every day, where dreams are born, and where student success is the norm. An appropriate heading over every agriculture classroom and lab door should be "A PLACE of LEARNING."

Career development events and leadership development events (commonly referred to as CDEs and LDEs by those in the agricultural education profession) are a major component of the FFA and agricultural education program. In theory, they simply support the fact the FFA is an integral and essential part of the agricultural education program. These CDEs/LDEs offer many potential benefits to agriculture teachers, students enrolled in agriculture classes and members of the FFA. Some of these anticipated benefits for students are as follows:

- Learn occupational or content skills which are needed to enter and succeed in the wide array of agricultural occupations.
- Learn essential life skills such as leadership, human relations and citizenship skills which will be beneficial in a wide array of occupations including agricultural occupations.
- Evaluate their achievements and learning. The performance of each student in these CDEs/LEDs will be the basis to determine their success. In addition, student performance will enable the agriculture teacher to determine the success of their teaching performance and make necessary revisions. Evaluation is one of the important steps in good teaching.
- Learn management and organizational skills. Planning, conducting, and evaluating CDEs/LDEs should involve students and provide worthwhile learning opportunities.
- A venue for students to receive positive and meaningful recognition, which is an excellent way for a teacher to motivate students to study and work hard to learn the subject matter being taught.

These benefits are being squandered in far too many programs and some of the reasons are as follows:

- Too many teachers place too much importance on winning at the district, regional and state level and these teachers believe, mistakenly in my opinion, that the best way to win is to work with a few of their more capable students, often out of class.

- In some cases, teachers spend an inordinate amount of class time on a particular subject area at the expense of many other important areas of instruction. In most cases, this is because there is a goal to prepare students to win at the higher level.
- Too often teachers of agriculture do not provide quality classroom instruction and utilize highly effective teaching methods designed to motivate students to reach their potential.
- Even though CDEs/LDEs can offer positive benefits for student learning, it has been my experience and observation that too often CDEs/LDEs are conducted in much a manner that provides little or no benefits for the vast majority of students and focuses on only a select few.

Several years ago, it became apparent to me that the agriculture profession was missing the great opportunity that competitive events (now called CDEs and LDEs) offered to increase student learning. In too many cases, the results of competitive events seemed to be more negative than positive. I was attending a banquet at the National FFA Convention in Kansas City and the speaker was rather boring. I took a pen and on the back of the banquet program began to write some ideas about how to maximize the positive benefits and minimize the negative aspects of competitive events. By the time I had finished, I had jotted down 17 thoughts about how competitive events should be conducted. I brought the list home and typed them with the title *Principles of Using Contests to Prepare Students for Careers in Agriculture*. In the next few pages, I will share these 17 principles and the rationale for them. They are almost exactly as I wrote them some 50 years ago. They are completely original. However, many other people are due credit for most of these principles including

Mr. Charles L. Eldridge, my high school agriculture teacher; Dr. Harold R. Binkley, my professor in the Master's level FFA course at the University of Kentucky; Dr. Ralph E. Bender, my professor for a doctoral level FFA course at The Ohio State University; my high school and university students, and my fellow agriculture teachers. Additionally, I learned a few ideas by observing the negative impacts on students from poor procedures used by others and myself. Perhaps, I came up with a couple of the principles on my own. These principles are a result of my experiences, education, and observations. All 17 of the principles can have a positive effect on student learning, but some are certainly more important than others. I consider the first three to be a must <u>with no compromise</u>:

1. Local CDEs/LDEs must be held.
2. CDEs/LDEs must be based upon the curriculum.
3. Instruction should precede each and every CDE/LDE.

Principle 1

CDEs/LDEs should be conducted at the local level.

CDEs/LDEs are of the utmost importance at the local level. It is at the local level that recognition for excellent performance is the most meaningful for students. It is where their parents, grandparents, neighbors, sweethearts, friends, teachers, and fellow classmates are. CDEs/LDEs are most valuable in motivating members to learn at the local level and decrease in value at the state and national levels.

At the local level, the teacher of agriculture is the giver of recognition to students. The teacher places

Great teachers are passionate about their subject.

the students on their shoulders and shows them off to the FFA chapter, the school, the parents and the community. However, the opposite tends to be true for the teachers. Unfortunately, it is somewhat rare for a teacher to receive much recognition from having held an outstanding local CDE/LDE. Teachers tend to receive their greatest recognition from their school administration, fellow schoolteachers, other agriculture teachers in the state, and even the state agricultural education director and state FFA advisor when their students achieve at the state or national level. It is imperative that the local teacher recognizes that the priority must be on the students in their classroom and the local CDEs/LDEs.

When a student does well in a local CDE/LDE, and this is reported by the local media, the byline leads with the name of the student. When that same student goes on and excels at the state level the same media headline will lead with local youth or the name of their school, omitting the student's name. When the same student goes on and excels at the national level the state media will stress the name of the state, i.e. Kentucky youth. At the local level, 100 percent of the students in the class where the subject matter is being taught can participate. At the district or regional level, that number falls to one in an individual event and, at best, a few more in team events.

It should be a rule that if a student did not participate in an instructionally related event at the local level, they are not eligible to participate at a higher level. Teachers should make local CDEs/LDEs the first priority in their planning, teaching and efforts.

Principle 1: Study/Review Questions

1. How do you rank CDEs/LDEs at the local, district, state, and national level in terms of their importance?
2. How do you justify your rankings?
3. At what level (local, state, or national) of CDEs/LDEs are students likely to receive the most meaningful recognition?
4. At what level (local, state, or national) are teachers likely to receive the most meaningful recognition?
5. Should teachers hold CDEs/LDEs at the local level which do not exist at the state or national level?
6. Should all students participate in a CDE/LDE being held in their class?

Principle 2

CDEs/LDEs conducted at the local level should be based upon the curriculum.

The curriculum should be based upon the needs and interests of the students in the agricultural education program. The curriculum should be one that prepares students for agricultural careers and to be college and career ready. Having a specific day to day performance–based curriculum is the most fundamental aspect of education. It is a huge mistake to base the instructional program on the CDEs/LDEs available at the state or national level. However, a program should conduct

Great teachers make class enjoyable—even fun.

CDEs/LDEs which are available at higher levels when they are congruent with the curriculum. A teacher should not even think that higher-level CDEs/LDEs are the only events that should be held at the local level. CDEs/LDEs should be a regular occurrence in the classroom, after all, CDEs/LDEs are an evaluation activity to see how well students have learned and measures how well the teacher has taught. Agriculture teachers should have many evaluation events (CDEs/LDEs) in their classrooms. An event can be held at the conclusion of almost every lesson or unit taught. For example, if tractor safety and operation is part of the curriculum in a class, a written safety test could be a local CDE and a tractor driving CDE could be held or they could be combined into one CDE such as Tractor Safety and Operation. If students are taught how to keep records, a CDE in a record keeping event could be held. The record keeping CDE could have two components, one being an application test of record keeping and the second based upon the records kept by the students on their SAE's. The format for CDEs/LDEs can take many avenues such as a performance test, oral report, written report, the production of a product, a written test, plus other opportunities, or some combination of these. The ideas of how to conduct a local level CDE/LDE based upon the instructional program are unlimited. Requiring that all CDEs/LDEs are an outgrowth of curriculum cannot be stressed enough. Surely, no teacher would expect students to take a classroom test on content that is not a part of the curriculum and has not been taught in the classroom.

> *Great teachers have relevant measurable lesson objectives.*

A Kentucky agriculture teacher had the first place team for three consecutive years in the state contest in small power equipment, but the following year he did not teach the appropriate class to hold a local CDE in small power equipment; therefore, his school neither held a local CDE nor entered the district CDE. The next six years after, he taught the class and had a state winning team each of these years. This same teacher has had a winning regional record keeping team for 23 years and has placed in the top five in the state in each of these years. He has shared that in each of these years he has several students in his freshman classes who could have done about as good in the regional contest as those who were on the team. He was consistent in teaching the entire class the same content and not just focusing on those selected to participate at the higher levels.

When CDEs/LDEs are tied to the course of study, a chapter may conduct CDEs/LDEs. Some of these events are held on a national level and some of which may exist at the state level only. However, many CDEs/LDEs can and should be conducted by the chapter at the local level only. In fact, local CDEs/LDEs should become a regular evaluation activity used as motivation in agriculture classrooms. In general, a chapter should not plan to enter any higher level CDE/LDE unless the appropriate subject matter has been taught and a local CDE/LDE has been held.

For many years I have believed it should be possible to hold at least 15 meaningful and relevant CDEs and LDEs based upon a year-long course of study in any area of agriculture. Today, I still believe it is possible to have that many and perhaps even more. A list of 16 teaching objectives for an instructional unit in vegetable gardening may be seen under the heading Instructional Unit on Vegetable Gardening which follows.

Instructional Unit on Vegetable Gardening

1. Determining the importance of growing a garden.
2. Selecting the garden site.
3. Preparing the site for planting.
4. Determining the vegetables to grow.
5. Selecting the varieties to grow.
6. Identifying the sources of seeds and plants.
7. Determining when to plant the different vegetables.
8. Determining the procedure of seeding and planting.
9. Supplying the needed fertilizer.

10. Controlling weeds in the garden.
11. Controlling insects in the garden.
12. Controlling diseases in the garden.
13. Providing water for the garden.
14. Harvesting the vegetables.
15. Using and/or marketing the vegetables.
16. Seeding the site with a cover crop.

A list of possible CDE activities related to vegetable gardening may be seen under the heading CDE Activities Related to the Instructional Unit on Vegetable Gardening which follows.

CDE Activities Related to the Instructional Unit on Vegetable Gardening

1. Identify four common garden weeds and four common garden insects from specimens and/or pictures.
2. List three major weeds that are a problem in many gardens and describe how to control them.
3. List three major insects that cause damage in many gardens and describe how to control them.
4. List three major diseases that cause damage in many gardens and describe how each damages a particular vegetable and what should be done to control the disease.
5. Identify four choices for a cover crop for a garden and indicate which you would choose and support your choice.
6. Identify one vegetable that you would grow in your garden; write a comprehensive report on the vegetable.
7. List at least six vegetables that can be planted/ seeded before the last frost and six vegetables that should be planted/seeded after the last frost.
8. Describe in detail the process of planting a tomato plant.

9. Provide advice (six facts) you would share with someone who has no gardening experience, but is thinking about growing a vegetable garden.
10. Make a vegetable garden plan that is 25' x 30' utilizing tomatoes, pole beans, beets, yellow squash, okra, corn, cucumbers, and one other vegetable of your choice. Include space devoted to each vegetable, row spacing, varieties selected, planting dates, and any other considerations you think appropriate to good gardening practices.

A creative teacher may want to combine, expand, modify, eliminate, or add other activities into their local vegetable gardening CDE. It is possible to conduct multiple CDEs on vegetable gardening.

Principle 2: Study/Review Questions

1. Should a teacher conduct CDEs/LDEs in areas which are not part of the curriculum?
2. Should a teacher try to prepare an individual or teams for all the CDEs/LDEs that are available at the state and national level? Why or why not?
3. How are CDEs/LDEs and student evaluation related?

Principle 3

Instruction should precede the local CDE/LDE.

Students should be taught the subject matter and/or the skills which are needed to do well in the CDE/LDE before the CDE/LDE is held. When students are taught well, they will look forward to being a participant in the CDE/LDE and they will eagerly look forward to the results as they will anticipate doing well. Many students do not like tests because they usually do not do well, and too often this is the result of little or no teaching of the test content. These same students, when taking a test with anticipated poor results, hope the results are never made known. In some cases, tests or pop quizzes are used as punishment when students are not working or behaving as the teacher believes they should. When a student expects to do well on a test, project, or report, they have been known to come back the next period after the evaluation to see if the teacher can tell them how they did. When students have been well taught, they can be expected to look forward to the CDE/LDE and even more importantly, they are likely to do well. The old expressions

Great teachers have students engaging in creative activities, problem solving, critical thinking and higher order learning skills.

that "success breeds success" and "successive success tends to make one successful" are so true. It is cruel to have students participate in an event at any level for which they have not been prepared. It is not criminal, but perhaps it should be. To be effective in teaching requires the planning of the lesson(s) and utilization of effective teaching methods. The job of the teacher is to produce desirable changes in behavior (learnings).

Appendix A and Appendix B are examples of processes to use local CDEs/LDEs as integral components of instruction. The first is tractor safety and operation, which I followed as a first-year teacher many years ago. The second is a more recent result of teaching a class of juniors how to prepare for an employment skills LDE. As a result, my grandson won the local, district and state LDE, and placed fifth in the nation with a gold rating. On occasion, a teacher will remark when their students do poorly at an advanced level, "my students didn't do well, but they did it on their own." This attitude misses the point of being a teacher.

Great teachers use class time productively.

Several years ago, I developed a record book and a series of instructional modules on record keeping. From these, I created a record keeping contest for freshmen students. There was a very high percent of participants throughout the state in the contest. Teams of three students participated in the district contests and all the record books were sent to the University of Kentucky to be scored. A combination of graduate and undergraduate students scored the record books. We received several books over the years with some interesting comments. I have selected one to share. On the front of the record book the student had written, "Please read inside of cover." On the inside of the cover the student wrote:

This student scored 5.4 out of a possible 100.

For a number of years, I was in charge of the FFA Seed ID and Seed Tag selection contest at the Kentucky State Fair. There would be 40 seeds in the seed ID part of the contest. These 40 seeds were taken from a list of 60 seeds in the State Fair catalog. Each year, I included corn and beans in the contest so that every student should be able to identify at least two seeds correctly. Each year, there would be one or two students who would correctly identify only two seeds, corn and beans. I suspect that any average student in high school, whether an agriculture student or not, could do as well. These students were supposed to be chapter winners in their school. I believe almost any teacher could take any average student in their program and instruct them for one hour or so, perhaps in the car while on the way to the fair, and they could do quite a bit better. A little instruction will go a long way.

As a first-year teacher, I put together seed kits and sets of seed tags; these had not existed prior to my arrival. I taught seed ID and seed tag selection for some five periods to my freshman class with 19 students. In the local contest five students tied for first place and we had to have a run-off to determine the student to represent our chapter at the state fair. The student placed first at state.

On the way home, the student remarked that "it was easier to win the state contest than the local contest." When asked how he had arrived at that conclusion, he remarked, "I originally tied with four of my classmates at home, but there was no tie in the state." I believe motivation and instruction is the key.

Great teachers have students reading, listening, writing, speaking, computing, and using technology skills.

During my first year of teaching, I scheduled 12 days on livestock selection and judging in a course for the sophomore class. There were 14 students enrolled in the class and none had any previous background or experience in showing or judging livestock. I had shown hogs and beef cattle at the county and district level but had never been on a livestock judging team nor had training in judging livestock. As a first-year teacher, I had to collect judging pictures to use in instruction and schedule field trips.

The instruction was continued for four nights during the summer with 100 percent of the students attending. The group also attended a couple of county fairs where there were strong livestock shows. That fall at the state fair the team placed first and went on to the national convention where they were a National Gold Emblem Livestock Judging Team. For several years, I assisted with registering judging teams at the state fair and almost every year members from a chapter would approach the registration table to ask what events were available. After being told, they would back away and decide who was entering each event. I have also had students come back after registering and change which event they would each participate in. One might conclude these students had been instructed in each of the events or that they had not been prepared for any of the events. I suspect the latter to be the case.

No student should be asked to participate in a local CDE/LDE for which they have not been taught, and no student or team should be taken to a higher level CDE/LDE unless they have had instruction in the event. To do so is teaching students that it is all right to be unprepared and perform poorly.

Similar results to those described in livestock judging and seed ID were attained in the land judging contest and the welding event. For the land judging contest, I taught the subject matter to the students in my junior class. Our chapter hosted a county wide contest in which the other five FFA chapters in the county participated. We secured the assistance of the District Soil Conservation Office to set up and conduct this event, which served as our local contest. The team members were motivated enough that they practiced on their own on a Sunday afternoon before the district event. The team went on to win the district, beating a chapter that had been the district winner for about 10 years, and placed third in the state contest.

The junior class was taught welding and a three-member team won the district contest and placed fourth in the

state contest. The team member scoring the highest at the state contest went on to be a welding instructor at the West Kentucky Technical School. The local contest was judged by the owner of the local welding supply house and the Murray State University Agriculture Mechanics Instructor. I must confess that several of the students in the class became better welders than their teacher, but I am not sure that they realized that. A couple of the students were utilized as teaching aides after their skill began to exceed that of the teacher.
Other contests such as tobacco grading, public speaking, creed speaking, and impromptu speaking were held in a manner similar to those already described. Today, I realize that several more local-only contests could have been held as other subjects were taught and student performance evaluated, but they were not conducted as a local CDE/LDE using the principles presented in this manuscript.

In my sophomore classes, I included a unit on tobacco grading. I made sure to teach it while the students were preparing their tobacco for market. We completed our local judging contest (our local CDE) a few days before the district FFA/4-H tobacco show and sale, so I called our county 4-H agent. There was a tobacco grading contest at the show and sale for both 4-H and FFA and I offered the 4-H agent the opportunity to use three of my students who were not in the top three of our FFA chapter but who were members of his 4-H club. He welcomed my students as his team. We did this both years I taught at Lowes High School and, in both of those years, my students placed first in both the FFA and the 4-H contest. No doubt the secret to success was motivation, instruction, and student learning.

Several years ago, I attended the FFA awards ceremony at the state fair, and when the state winning team of the coveted livestock judging contest was announced I noticed where they were seated. After the ceremony, I approached the students from the winning team and asked what grade they were in. Each one had just finished their sophomore year. When I asked how they learned to judge livestock they said they learned it in their agriculture class the past year. At that time livestock judging in the state was usually taught in the sophomore year.

When students enter an advanced level CDE/LDE multiple times, other students are being denied that opportunity for that experience. When this happens, the emphasis has shifted from motivating students to learn the instructional content to a desire to do well at the advanced levels.

Principle 3: Study/Review Questions

1. How much responsibility does the teacher have that students do well when participating in CDEs/LDEs?
2. What should a teacher do to inspire and motivate students to be eager to participate in a class CDE/LDE?

Principle 4

Students should know about the CDE/LDE at the time the instruction begins.

If the CDE/LDE is to provide motivation for the students, it is imperative that the students know about the CDE/LDE at the start of the instruction. This initial information should spell out the lessons that will be taught, what the students will be expected to know and/or do, and what performance levels the students will need to reach to receive recognition. No student is motivated by something unknown.

Great teachers inspire students to dream big.

Once I heard a teacher tell a class that they were having a test, and the students had not been told because the teacher wanted it to be "fair" to all the students. It is a lot more "fair" if students are told in advance and a lot more motivating if everyone knows at the time the instruction begins.

Principle 4: Study/Review Questions

1. Why should students know about an upcoming
   CDE/LDE at the time instruction begins?
2. Why do some students have the attitude that tests may
   be punishment?

Principle 5

Information on recognition and awards should be shared.

Virtually all human beings like to receive recognition. Recognition and awards can be used to motivate students to learn the content. Again, it is essential that information about the recognition and or awards be made known to the students at the beginning of instruction leading to the evaluation activity of the CDE/LDE. To learn of the recognition awards after the instruction provides no motivation for learning. If members are to receive plaques, ribbons, certificates, or other awards for excellent performance in the CDE/LDE, it is good psychology to allow the member to see and handle the awards.

The prerequisite for student motivation is a motivated teacher.

Hopefully, many of them will make personal commitments to learn so they can perform at the required level to receive recognition or an award.

During my first year of teaching a representative of *Progressive Farmer Magazine* came to my school and shared with my freshmen class the marketing program for the magazine. He started with the smaller prizes for selling, such as a pocketknife, and then larger prizes like an automatic 16-gauge shotgun. He brought all of these items to let the class see and hold them. (Needless to say, these sorts of items couldn't be brought into the school today!) The students sold an unbelievable amount of magazines and received an astounding number of the prizes. One student sold enough magazines that he received almost one of all the available prizes. I have always thought that agricultural educators should be as skilled at motivating students as the *Progressive Farmer Magazine* salesperson.

Principle 5: Study/Review Questions

1. Why should students know about recognition/awards associated with the CDE/LDE when the instruction begins?
2. On the front end of instruction, how important is it that students actually see/touch/handle awards they may receive? Why is this so?

Principle 6

Rules and procedures should be based upon local needs rather than state or national requirements.

Too often, a local chapter takes a look at the state CDEs/LDEs rules and procedures and adopts them as-is for the local chapter. Often the state rules are identical to the national, and when this is the case, we are expecting students at the local level to perform exactly as those students who advance and compete at the national level. This practice does not make sense from an educational or motivational standpoint. It is not reasonable to expect all the local members to perform at the level of the national participants. In the case of prepared public speaking, this may mean that students at the local level are expected to write and give public speeches with a duration of six to eight minutes. Such requirements are almost certain to suppress and limit participation of many students and is too much to expect of most of the members at the local level. It would be more realistic to set the time limit for the local prepared speech LDE from two to four minutes, and then work with the local winner to further develop and expand the speech for the higher level LDE.

Great teachers are positive role models.

National rules are usually determined by a highly competent committee that likely has representatives that include an outstanding agriculture teacher/ FFA advisor, a national student officer, a state staff person and a member of the national staff. Even though these rules may be appropriate for the national CDEs/LDEs, they likely are not what is best for students at the local level. Local rules should be set at the local level. Of course, it is alright to review the higher level CDEs/LDEs rules, but in many cases the rules should be modified for use at the local level. It is just as reasonable that not all state rules should be identical to the national rules.

> *Great teachers inspire students to aspire.*

Rules and procedures at the local level should encourage and motivate students to participate and learn. Even though the following two examples are not related to agriculture, they are excellent illustrations of how using national requirements may not be the best at the local level. When my son was six years old, we joined a newly established tribe of Y-Indian Guides of other six-year-old boys and their fathers. The Y-Indian Guides organization was sponsored by the YMCA. My Indian name was "Big Feather" and my son was "Little Feather." The six aims and purposes of the organization were spelled out in the official handbook. At the organizational meeting, it had been announced that any young brave who recited the aims would receive their first feather for their headband. I changed most of the aims to be a better fit for a six-year-old who at the time hardly knew his ABC's let alone how to read. The aim of "love the sacred circle of my family" became "love your mom and dad" and the aim of "seek and preserve the beauty of Our Creator's work in forest, field and stream" became "don't litter" as the anti-litter movement was quite strong at that time.

At the first meeting, the father serving as chief of our tribe asked what little brave was ready to stand and recite the aims to receive their first feather. My son was seated next to me on a couch and, after a couple of elbow jabs from me, he went to the front and stood with his head down and hesitantly recited the aims as I had taught him. The chief who held the "talking stick" announced that my son had not gotten the aims correctly; therefore, the members were silent and there was no war hoop of approval. My son sat back down by me and placed a couple elbow jabs into my side along with a couple of muted sobs. When the meeting was over and we got to our car, he began to cry and asked why he didn't get his feather. I responded by telling him it was my fault, that I had changed the aims to what I considered a more appropriate wording for a brand-new YMCA tribe of six-year-old boys. I still believe I was right. However, obviously most of the fathers, who were well-educated, felt the wording of the national aims should be our wording.

The second example involved my daughter when she was a first-year member of the Acteens, a young girls group in our Southern Baptist church. She did a lot of work to receive her first degree and kept excellent records of her activities in her book. A couple of days before the award ceremony she found out she would not be getting her degree because she had kept her book written rather than typed. The Southern Baptist Convention rules from Nashville specified books should be typed. Understandably, she was disappointed and hurt. Regardless, she attended the coronation ceremony, and after the ceremony we went to Fellowship Hall for refreshments and to see the girl's application books. My daughter's book was not on display, and she remarked, even though her book was not typed as the Southern Baptist Convention said it should be, she thought her book should have still been displayed for people to see. At that time, I believed she should have received her degree and had her degree book placed on display. I still do. After that, she dropped out of Acteens and never again participated. Local CDE/LDE rules do not have to duplicate state or national CDE/LDE rules, state CDE/LDE rules do not have to duplicate national CDE/LDE rules, and most of the time, they should not.

Principle 6: Study/Review Questions

1. Is it a good idea for the teacher to adopt the state and/or national rules for their local CDEs/LDEs? Why?
2. Who should set the "ground rules" for local CDEs/LDEs?

Principle 7

Most CDEs/LDEs should be limited to the instructional related class(es).

If a given CDE/LDE is to have maximum impact on motivating students, the participants in the CDE/LDE should be limited to those students enrolled in the class engaged in the study of the instructional unit related to the CDE/LDE. This utilizes motivation at its best and ensures the CDE/LDE is truly instructionally related. For example, if livestock judging is taught at the sophomore class level, or in a livestock class, the participants should be limited to those students studying livestock judging. There are other CDEs/LDEs that would fall in other specific instructional classes. If students from other classes participate you tend to reduce the motivation and learning of those students in the

Great teachers share real life stories.

class that matches the CDE/LDE. When there is more than one class being taught the same subject matter, the approach should be to hold class CDEs/LDEs and then have the better students from each class compete in a chapter CDE/LDE. An example of when all students might compete in the same CDE/LDE would be the record book CDE, but even then, a grade level/class level CDE would be most appropriate and the best from each grade/class could go on to compete in the chapter CDE. Allowing advanced students to repeatedly participate may give the chapter a stronger representative, but it will reduce the learning and motivation in the students who are currently being instructed in the subject matter.

Principle 7: Study/Review Questions

1. Why should student participation in CDEs/LDEs be limited to the classes where the related instruction is provided?
2. What are some examples where it could be desirable to have a CDE/LDE across grade level classes and how should these CDEs/LDEs be structured?

Principle 8

Students should earn the right to represent their chapter at advanced levels.

The teacher should not be the one who selects the students to enter the CDEs/LDEs at the higher levels, as the chapter representatives should be selected by their performance. Students should have earned the right based upon their performance in the local CDE/LDE. Members who have earned the right will be the strongest participants to represent your chapter. Experience indicates that teachers/advisors do not always select the best representatives regardless of how good their intentions may be. Another real plus occurs when members earn the right to represent their organization. They can be expected to go and participate and not back out at the last minute. A word of caution: when students earn the right, it will also become difficult for the teacher to decide not to take the students, and should this happen, parents will likely complain to the school's administration. However, when the teacher has invested time in teaching and holding a local CDE/LDE, they will be almost 100 percent certain to take students to the higher-level

Great teachers help students have successive successful experiences.

CDE/LDE. In fact, likely the chapter will participate even if it must hitch-hike to get there!

When one of my students named Junior made the livestock judging team, the entire class, including me, was surprised. I would have never picked Junior to be a member of the team. Junior was the only child of older parents. In school, he had never distinguished himself in any way and he was not one to participate in most activities. He wore big legged jeans (Washington Dee Cee brand) when tight legged jeans were the students' preferred choice (Levi Strauss brand). After he made the livestock judging team, his

Great teachers have high expectations for their students.

mother came to school to tell me that Junior had shared that he planned to go to the state fair in Louisville and participate in the state FFA livestock judging contest. She said his dad would not let him go. He was afraid Junior might get hurt on the 300-mile trip. It was then I understood why Junior had often expressed a safety concern about participating in activities. She asked if I would come to their home and talk with his father, and I agreed. I don't recall what I said to his father, but Junior got to go. I didn't know it then, but later I learned Junior's dad was 77 years old at that time.

I can still see Junior when he found out our team had won the state livestock judging contest. I never had to talk to his dad about Junior going to Kansas City. I suspect Junior was going to Kansas City regardless of what his dad might have said. Some 48 years later, at a school FFA reunion luncheon, Junior pulled his national FFA gold emblem medallion for livestock judging out of his pocket for me to see. In the same class, Gary was one of the strongest academic students I have ever taught. Gary did not make the team. Had

I been picking the team he would have been my number one pick. Gary went on to get a Ph.D. in biochemistry from Duke University, and he later told me, in a letter, that he completed 83 hours of college chemistry in his program. He also wrote that he never developed the skills in class to be able to tell one hog's butt from another. However, Gary was elected to serve as chapter secretary, and he received second place in the state with his Secretary's Book. The year after I left, he served as chapter president, senior class president, and was valedictorian of his graduating class.

My first year as a teacher I had five students in the freshman class tie for first place in the chapter Seed ID and Seed Tag Contest, but only one could enter the state contest held at the state fair. Since the five students were freshman, it was almost 300 miles to the state fair, and our chapter had been in existence only one year (we received our charter during my first year), we had almost no tradition of success and no funds to help pay the students expenses. I told the students to check with their parents to see if they would be able to attend the state fair, but I guessed that most would not be able to go. Was I wrong! The next morning, before classes started, I had five students waiting at the agriculture building door reporting that they were good to go. I set up a tie breaker to determine the eventual winner.

When I am told by a teacher that some of their students cancelled or didn't show, I always wonder how hard the students had worked to earn the privilege of representing their chapter and how effective the teacher had been teaching the students.

Principle 8: Study/Review Questions

1. How should individuals or team members who will represent a chapter at the district or state level in a CDE/LDE be selected?
2. What are some potential problems when the teacher makes the selection?

Principle 9

Achievement should be measured against a standard of performance rather than between individuals.

Instead of pitting our members against each another, it is much more motivating to have members compete against a preset standard of performance(s). For example, in a record book CDE, members should compete against the standard of an excellent record book, which involves neatness, completeness, accuracy, up-to-date records, and so forth, rather than competing for first place. In a weed identification CDE, a predetermined number of weeds would need to be correctly identified. Usually, when first place is the goal, perhaps at best three students are motivated. Oftentimes, the student likely to place first is known by all the students before the instruction begins. Some may recognize the top three performances, and this may increase member motivation for only two or three additional students. When a standard is used the number of students who are motivated to do well likely will increase many times. In fact, it is possible that every student might be motivated to be a winner.

At the Kentucky FFA Leadership Center, each chapter's

Great teachers evaluate teacher and student performance.

cottage is inspected each day of the week. On the last day of camp, chapters who meet the pre-set standard receive a blue-ribbon cottage award. There is no first-place award. Almost all the chapters receive this award. The chapter's members go to considerable effort in keeping and preparing their cottages to receive an excellent score. In fact, it is not uncommon to see a chapter member sweeping the roof of their cottage. However, if the policy was to recognize the best, a few chapters likely would go to the extreme by hanging pictures, having official FFA towels, wash cloths, containers, bed spreads, and so on in order to win first place. On the other hand, some chapters would decide not to compete, and many would only make a minimum effort to keep their cottages clean and orderly. Student leaders at the Kentucky Leadership Training Center are recognized each week, and the number of members that can be recognized is not limited. The church youth camp that my children attended recognized the boy and girl camper of the week, but the approach the FFA uses is far better. In many cases, it is not necessary to have a first-place winner and is far better to have a bunch of winners. A chapter may have one standard level to determine excellence, or a chapter could have more than one level, such as gold, silver, and bronze.

Principle 9: Study/Review Questions

1. How many performance levels of student recognition should CDEs/LDEs provide?
2. Why is recognizing level(s) of performance a better approach than recognizing only the best?

Principle 10

CDEs/LDEs should be designed so that all who excel can be recognized.

In all CDEs/LDEs, students who achieve a predetermined standard of performance should be recognized. I would prefer recognizing all students who excelled and reached the desired level of competency. The chapter can still select the student or students to represent the chapter in the district or the state CDE/LDE, but CDE/LDE designed as described might provide recognition for 10-12 students or more out of the 16 who may be enrolled in the class. The CDE/LDE, so designed, could possibly motivate all of the students enrolled in the class to

Great teachers are givers of recognition.

improve their skills/learning. Compare such an approach to only three or four motivated when only the best, or the three best, are recognized. Most local CDEs/LDEs should be recognized in a similar manner. Recognizing those who fail to reach the desired level of competency as a participant is also a possibility.

Principle 10: Study/Review Questions

1. What should the criteria be to recognize students participating in CDEs/LDEs?
2. Should there be one level of standard for recognition or more than one level?

Principle 11

A wide variety of recognition and awards can and should be utilized.

Generally, recognition for achievement in CDEs/LDEs is more important than any tangible awards a student may receive. However, awards can be an important, meaningful, and lasting symbol of student achievement. Some examples of effective, and rather inexpensive awards are ribbons, certificates, plaques, pins, medals, and trophies. Of course, recognition can also be provided in ways other than tangible hardware. Some examples are announcing winners at chapter meetings and having them stand in the front of the meeting room for applause, through bulletin board displays, letters to parents, a smile and handshake,

Great teachers make use of positive recognition.

a fist bump, a thumbs up, newsletters, school intercom announcements, local newspaper articles/photos, or newsletters and school board meetings. The chapter should use many different means to provide recognition and/or awards during the year. Some key CDEs/LDEs may have permanent plaques with the winners' names engraved each year and displayed in the chapter's glassed-in case, on the classroom wall and/or on a wall in the school hallway.

My mother-in-law received her first certificate after she was well past 65 years of age. The certificate was from the University of Kentucky for displaying her afghans at a hobby/craft show and she had it framed and proudly displayed it on the family room wall of her home. A couple of years later my father-in-law received his first certificate for having the yard of the month in his town. When his daughter asked if he wanted to have the certificate framed and put on the wall adjacent to her mother's certificate, her mother quickly responded that he didn't. Apparently, mom didn't want to share the recognition that she had! However, when pressed, he said, "yes he did," and his certificate was framed and hung on the wall.

A teacher mentioned to me that he had sent a congratulatory letter to parents of students who had excelled in a particular local CDE. A couple of days later, a student reported he had almost been in trouble when his dad picked up the mail that afternoon and saw the letter from the school. Before opening the letter, his dad had wanted to know what kind of trouble his son was in at school. Upon opening and reading the letter he was pleasantly surprised, because unfortunately, most of the time a letter or email message from the school means there is a problem with attendance, behavior, or poor performance.

One of my former students also informed me that his chapter had developed a certificate to present at chapter meetings to the freshmen who had successfully recited the FFA creed. At the chapter meeting, those who had recited the creed received their certificate. Immediately after the meeting, three members who hadn't recited the creed approached the teacher and asked if they could still say the creed and get a certificate. He said they could, and one of the students asked if he could recite it immediately. When the teacher said yes, he promptly recited the creed and received his certificate. The other two successfully recited the creed a few days later. The teacher learned the motivational power of a simple certificate. Too many people have never received a positive tangible symbol of recognition for their achievements.

Principle 11: Study/Review Questions

1. What forms of recognition and awards do think best for students participating in CDEs/LDEs?
2. What CDEs/ LDEs in your chapter might be important enough to merit a permanent plaque with names of winners engraved each year?
3. In order to motivate your students to excel, what new traditions, awards, or recognition would work well in your chapter?

Principle 12

Only excellent performance should be recognized.

As someone so aptly put it, "When performance is poor, more instruction is needed – not recognition." When a member is recognized who does not merit it, the recognition is cheapened. In the same vein, chapter members must not castigate members who have done poorly by publicly recognizing their poor performance. When a member has done poorly no recognition is the best recognition. There is no place in the FFA chapter to give members "black ribbons." I still remember the Beetle Bailey cartoon when Beetle was lying in his bunk with Sarge telling him, "when I give you recognition, you still complain." On the headboard of Beetle's bunk was a large banner with the words, "Goof-off of the Month."

Great teachers use effective teaching methods.

Many summers as part of our church youth activities my own children attended a week long overnight camp. The camp director had a unique way of recognizing the housekeeping of each cabin. Each day the campers that had both the very best and also the very worst kept cabin were awarded a special ribbon. It was my observation that some cabins were in fact highly motivated to receive the "black ribbon" award. When I visited the camp one year on Parent Night one of the youth told me with a real sense of pride that her cabin had won the black ribbon that day. She went on to explain that to earn the black ribbon they really had to work hard creating a huge and maybe even a creatively staged mess in their cabin. Clearly, great teachers encourage their students to strive for "blue ribbons."

It took some effort, a few years ago, to convince the state leadership in agricultural education that we should not list the names of all participants and chapters from first to last in all our state fair events. Having students line up, or be announced from first to last, is very humiliating and should never be done. Some of them near last place might even cry; others will laugh it off. Adults would never stand for it. Of course, if the principles outlined in this manuscript are followed, that will never happen.

Several years ago, I attended an FFA parent member banquet where awards were being presented for many different activities. A member presented the rabbit award and read the achievements of the winning project while the recipient stood in front of the audience. The last line of the presentation was "bad luck set in and all his rabbits died." Perhaps, the rabbit award should have been cancelled.

Principle 12: Study/Review Questions

1. How should students who do poorly in CDEs/LDEs
    be recognized?
2. What level of performance will serve best as your
    threshold for students to receive positive
    recognition?

Principle 13

Recognition and awards should be presented in such a way, and at such a time, as to make the recognition meaningful.

The when, where, and how in recognizing students is as important as the award itself, often more so. In general, awards or recognition should be presented soon after the CDE/LDE. If a welding CDE is held after school on Thursday, the ribbons (if ribbons are being used) may be presented immediately after the contest. Recipients of the top awards can be announced and receive applause at the next chapter meeting, and all the participants can be asked to stand for applause. Too many chapters fail to make effective use of presenting recognition and awards at regular meetings. Member recognition should be a significant part of each chapter meeting. Names of the award winners can be posted on the bulletin board and submitted to the school newspaper, and a picture of the winner(s), along with the names of all the contestants receiving an excellent rating, can be put in the local newspaper. Only the top award recipient(s) of the various CDEs/LDEs should be held over for the local award banquet. If all awards are held for the banquet, your banquet may become a marathon lasting too long with some of the recognition losing its effectiveness. A banquet program insert can be prepared, which lists award winners for the year in addition to those being recognized at the banquet. In fact, a banquet insert may be six pages, or even more, filled with names of those who excelled in CDEs/LDEs, as well as those who excelled or participated in community service, leadership, fund-raising and other chapter activities.

Great teachers care about their students and their students know it.

When my daughter was a third grader, her school held a Captain Tag look alike drawing contest. Captain Tag was the traffic officer who flew his helicopter over our city during afternoon rush hour reporting on traffic accidents and which streets were backed up. My daughter was selected as the school winner, and it was announced by Captain Tag himself by landing his helicopter on the school lawn as the student body awaited his arrival. He exited his copter, announced the winner, and presented my daughter with a Captain Tag t-shirt. The recognition was handled in an awesome way. In almost all cases, the recognition is more meaningful than the award. The award is symbolic of the achievement. In general, awards of a nature that can be kept over time and displayed are better than those which have a short life.

Principle 13: Study/Review Questions

1. When and where do you think recognition for successful participation in CDEs/LDEs should be presented?
2. What is the importance of providing recognition to members who have excelled in fundraising, community service, academic achievement, and chapter activities?

Principle 14

Several frequent, small, or moderate awards are superior to a few larger awards.

Studies in psychology indicate that it is more effective to motivate members by giving several small or moderate awards frequently than to occasionally give fewer larger awards. This is to say, more motivation will result from investing $200.00 in ribbons and certificates and distributing them during the year to members for excellent performance in different CDEs/LDEs, than by buying a couple of large plaques and giving them to the two most outstanding members (the best) at the end of the school year. In most cases, chapters do not

Great teachers are passionate about teaching.

have the financial resources to give awards of substantial means, nor is it necessary to motivate students. In most cases, awards become tokens of the student's achievement. Bridge players all over the country strive to get another point or even a partial point toward another level of achievement. For many, this is an ongoing effort for many years, often for a lifetime. We can use this knowledge of human behavior when we set up our awards/recognition program to motivate and enhance learning in our classrooms.

Principle 14: Study/Review Questions

1. Do you think it is important to provide expensive awards to participants in CDEs/LDEs? Why?
2. What is potentially gained by spreading recognition/awards over the entire year as opposed to presenting them all at the end of the year banquet or program?

Principle 15

Selection of winners should involve students, graduated members, alumni members, community members and outside experts.

Many local CDEs/LDEs can and should utilize members in the selection process, particularly at the elimination or class level. If students are properly oriented and challenged, they will be excellent judges. In conducting a local creed speaking LDE, the chapter can conduct a class LDE with students in the class serving as judges to determine those who receive an excellent rating and those to advance and compete in the chapter finals. By having classmates serve as judges, and using a standard score card, the weaker students are much more likely to be willing participants. For the chapter LDE, the committee in charge can bring in alumni members, school officials, personnel from industry, business, and agriculture to serve as judges. The use of such people will be good public relations, will be impressive to the contestants and membership, and should ensure a wise choice to represent the organization in the district or state LDE. By screening the participants, the chapter does not "show off" some of the poorer performers, and at the same time lightens the workload of the outside judges, besides letting the students have a meaningful experience in making the initial selections. The fact that classmates have selected the students to advance to chapter level makes it almost certain that those selected students will have the confidence to participate in the chapter event before outside judges.

When my first chapter record book contest was held, the committee took all the student record books to the person whom they had selected to judge the books. The judge did a thorough job of scoring the books and selecting those that met the standard of excellence, as well as the best book for each class level and the chapter. However, he also wrote a nice letter suggesting that we screen the books in the future and only send the better books to be judged. He indicated having a committee screen the books of members would be a good experience for the members and also would considerably lighten the workload of the judge. We took his advice the next year.

Great teachers create masterpieces in their classrooms.

When my students held the chapter dairy impromptu speaking contest it was judged by the field person from our local Pet Milk Company. Our welding contest was judged by the owner of our local welding supply business and the agriculture welding instructor at our regional college. The local production farm credit manager was the judge for our tractor driving contest. Our land judging contest was conducted by the soil conservation field person. Prepared public speaking and creed speaking were judged by a combination of community leaders and school personnel. Woodworking projects were judged by a member of the adult agriculture class, a local tobacco grader graded the samples of tobacco used in the chapter grading contest, and a retired teacher of agriculture served as the judge for the record book contest. The seed and grain store owner prepared the seed tags used in the Seed ID and Seed Tag Contest.

An excellent hog breeder in an adjoining county, who had helped us secure some show and breeding animals, sent a note a few days after attending our banquet in which he stated that he had been an active supporter of the FFA for many years but it was the first banquet he had ever been invited to attend.

After my first banquet as a teacher, the editor and publisher of our local newspaper remarked he had attended a lot of FFA banquets (he held the state honorary degree and we had six FFA chapters in the county), but he had never seen so many community and agricultural leaders in attendance and he wondered why they were there. The answer was that these people had been involved in the program in a variety of ways, primarily by assisting with and judging CDEs/LDEs.

Asking people to help with CDEs/LDEs is a way to build support for the agriculture program and the teacher and, best of all, they will help make the program better.

Sometimes, young teachers may be reluctant or hesitant to ask people for help. However, it has been my experience that almost all people are willing to be involved with the school. It is in my opinion that the agriculture community, and community at large, wants to be involved with the agriculture/FFA program. In general, they consider it an honor to help the school, the teacher, and the students.

Here is one last story on how willing individuals will be to assist the teacher and chapter. In the fall of my first year of teaching, I heard a knock on my classroom door. When I opened the door, an older gentleman was standing in the doorway with his hand extended to me. He told me his name was Miles Meridith and he handed me his business card. He asked if he could come in and talk with me for a few minutes after my class was dismissed, and I said yes. When the class was over, he asked what we would be having to eat at our banquet in the spring and, if we would be having grilled/barbecued chicken, he would be glad to prepare it for us. Not prone to accept an offer from a total stranger to fix food for our banquet, I told Mr. Meridith that should the students decide to have chicken I would get in contact with him. Truthfully, we had already talked about having barbecued chicken, but I thought it best to handle his offer the way I did. A few days later, I showed my principal Mr. Meridith's card and told him of Mr. Meridith's offer. My principal told me Mr. Meridith had been the school superintendent of an adjoining county, and after that he was the head of the Chamber of Commerce in the same county where he still lived. He further told me he was well known for barbecuing chicken.

A few weeks later I shared this with my high school agriculture teacher. He said Mr. Meridith was great at barbecuing chicken, and I was really lucky he had offered to do our banquet. He said that for years he had grilled chickens at the regional FFA awards banquet, and that Mr. Meridith had started his career as a teacher of agriculture in a different part of the state.

I called Mr. Meridith to see what his charge would be. He told me there would be no charge for his services and indicated he would get the chickens and charcoal wholesale. He would make the sauce from scratch at no charge and, if we wanted baked beans, he would make those from scratch, which would save us money. The deal sounded better all the time. He did, however, have a few requirements: 1) he would need about six students to assist him with the cooking; 2) he wanted to be invited to attend the banquet; 3) he would like to put a couple of extra chickens on the grill, which he would freeze for his next fishing trip, but he would deduct the cost from our bill; and 4) he would like to come to my freshmen class the week of the banquet and teach a lesson on how chickens should be barbecued. A deal was struck.

Mr. Meridith was a great teacher, and he told the class that he had already barbecued over a million birds and was working on his second million. He taught using the problem-solving method. As I mentioned earlier, he had been a teacher of agriculture early in his career. Our banquet was on Saturday night and I was having trouble getting all the six students lined up as he had requested. He told the class that doing the cooking would be a tough job as they would have to do quite a bit of sampling to make sure each batch of chicken was cooked just right, and still eat their half chicken at the banquet that night. After his lesson, he got several commitments from the class to help. He even agreed to pick up a couple of students who needed a ride.

I can still see Mr. Meridith when he arrived in his truck around noon with the two students he had picked up beside him and the truck bed filled with boxes of chickens, bags of charcoal, five-gallon lard cans, a bag of dried beans, and grill racks. The students later told me, during the afternoon, Mr. Meridith sat in a director's chair, directed the process, and shared stories with the students. He shared World War I stories, and he showed the students his war wounds. What a great experience! He did a repeat performance the next year, and I still have, and use, his sauce recipe of five ingredients and "NO OTHER JUNK." I wonder to this day why he chose to come to my classroom. I wish I had asked.

Principle 15: Study/Review Questions

1. How can students be best utilized in helping judge CDEs/LDEs?
2. Who are people in your school that would make excellent judges for your CDEs/LDEs?
3. Who in your community would make excellent judges for your CDEs/LDEs?

Principle 16

Students should plan, carry out, and evaluate CDEs/LDEs with the supervision of the teacher.

In many of the chapter CDEs/LDEs, the members should play a significant role in planning, conducting, and evaluating the event. This involvement will develop member planning, organizational, and leadership skills. Having members involved will increase their buy-in of CDEs/LDEs and get members "out of the stands," "off of the bench," and "on to the playing floor." In essence, members can become teacher's aides, which can increase the teacher's impact on the instructional program. The teacher must realize the need for orienting members, for keeping check on their progress, and offering advice and guidance at certain critical times. With each graduating class, a teacher who has involved their students in the CDEs/LDEs can make the following lament: "Just when my students really know what and how to operate, they go and graduate, and I have to start all over with a new group." Such is the job of the teacher.

Great teachers make effective use of questions.

Principle 16: Study/Review Questions

1. How can you use students to help conduct your local CDEs/LDEs?
2. What will be the benefits to both students and the teacher of having students involved in planning and conducting CDEs/LDEs?

Principle 17

The goal/purpose of CDEs/LDEs should be student learning, not winning district, state and/or national CDEs/LDEs.

CDEs/LDEs should be used as a vehicle to promote learning. Teaching is our calling. Education is a teacher's process and learning is a teacher's product. Winning, being the best or first at advanced levels, is a nice by-product. The teacher's goal must be for the members to learn sound agricultural, leadership and citizenship skills and to have multiple winners in a plethora of local CDEs/LDEs. Teachers may depart from sound principles of teaching if their number one priority is winning at advanced levels. It is my judgment that conducting CDEs/LDEs the "right" way is the only way to go and the results will prove astonishing. In fact, teachers who effectively implement the 17 principles presented in this manuscript will be successful at all levels – local, district, state and national. Agriculture classrooms will truly become a place for high levels of learning for all the students in the class.

The gulf is great, perhaps unfathomable between the mediocre and the great teacher.

Principle 17: Study/Review Questions

1. How well do you think students will do in higher level CDEs/LDEs who come from schools where the 17 principles listed and discussed in this manuscript are followed?
2. As a teacher, how do you define winning?

Summary

CDEs/LDEs in your chapter can be a vehicle for motivating members to learn and they will contribute much to members becoming technically competent. However, if CDEs/LDEs are to have a positive influence and are to make the maximum contribution to the agriculture program, they must be carefully selected and properly conducted using sound educational principles. Unless based on sound principles, CDEs/LDEs can be, and often are, detrimental to students learning and their development. The slogan should not be "how to win," but "how to increase desirable learning on the part of the students."

Many outstanding chapters have found that utilizing the above principles will result in a large number of excellent performances and significantly more than a fair share of winners at the district, state, and even national level.

The implementation of these principles will require very skilled teachers of agriculture; teachers who care a lot about themselves – so they can care about their students. These are the teachers who think in terms of putting their students on their shoulders and showing them off to others, rather than standing on the shoulders of their students so they may be seen. First, they must have a goal to have their students succeed, to experience success, and to have that good feeling – like being on the south side of the barn out of the north wind on a cold windy winter day when a bright sun is shining on their back. Second, they must care about their school and community and they must want to serve it. Third, they must care about the agriculture program and the FFA. They must believe both are important, that every day in class must be productive, and that every classroom minute should be utilized to teach agriculture and leadership. And fourth, they must care about the students whom they teach. They must believe that each student is valuable and that each student has potential waiting to be developed.

One of the strong aspects of CDEs/LDEs is that there can be a wide array of knowledge and skills tested. In my program, I had students with a wide range of academic abilities and interests. Gary, who excelled in academics, went on to get a Ph.D. from Duke University. He retired at a rather young age as a vice president in charge of international sales for a major company with a salary some two and one-half times my highest salary. Gary didn't make the livestock judging team or the welding team, but he had the second place FFA Secretary's Book in the state. He was a state winner in the Seed ID contest, and he served as president of the chapter his senior year. Bill, on the other hand, was not a strong academic student, but he made the welding team that placed fourth in the state. He was also the winner of the chapter tractor driving event. Bill became a successful farmer in the community.

CDEs/LDEs in the agricultural education program can and should focus on a wide content area such as flower arranging, developing a farm or business plan, controlling diseases or insects in crops and livestock, developing a soil and water conservation plan, operating a tractor, constructing a fence, figuring returns from an enterprise, identifying trees, basic electrical skills, grooming and showing a steer, public speaking skills, conducting a meeting, sales skills, laying out an irrigation plan, preparing for a job interview, and caring for bees. The list of possibilities is almost limitless, and there are almost certain to be CDEs/LDEs to match the interest and ability of all students, so the field is wide open for a creative teacher. Students like Gary and Bill, and many, many others, can find their place in the sun and, as a result, have a productive career and successful life.

I wish I could say that successful implementation of these CDE/LDE principles is easy. It is not! However, it can be great fun and very rewarding. If done properly, the sign over the agriculture classroom and laboratory doors, "A PLACE of LEARNING," will be brightly shining.

Appendix A

Conducting a Local CDE in Tractor Safety and Operation
Tractor Safety and Operation CDE

Introduction

Before beginning instruction on tractor safety and operation the students will be told what lessons will be taught, and that a CDE will be held at the conclusion of the instruction. Students will be told the standard(s) of performance required to be recognized at the next FFA meeting and will be shown the certificate that they will receive. The winner will also receive a model tractor with an engraved plate indicating first place in the CDE. This CDE will be conducted in the freshmen class if the school has a freshmen class, if not, it will be part of the introductory Agricultural Mechanics Class.

Lessons to Be Taught

1) How important is the safe operation of a tractor?

Students will use the computer to find information on the number of farm accidents with particular emphasis on those that are related to the operation of tractors and machinery. Also, they will be directed to find the reasons why farming is a hazardous occupation and how agriculture/farming is ranked as a hazardous occupation. The teacher will lead the class to come to the conclusion that the safe operation of a tractor is very important in preventing accidents and human injury and, in some cases, death of the operator.

2) What are the safety features of operating a tractor?

Students will have to read and list the safety features of operating a tractor. The class will arrive at a conclusion using teacher directed discussion to compile a list of safety features. Each student will list at least five of these features, which are the most important to them, and write a justification for each feature they choose. The teacher will grade their responses, and this will be part of the rubric on the CDE.

3) How should a tractor be operated?

Using a tractor, the teacher will demonstrate to the class all aspects of how to operate a tractor. It is very important this is covered thoroughly, as students will then be allowed to start and drive the tractor with close teacher supervision. Students will be given ample opportunity for practice. The teacher may want to have a couple of adult farmers present to assist with supervision.

4) How should the tractor course be driven?

At this point, the tractor driving course will be set up and a single axle trailer will be placed behind the tractor. Since this is a local CDE, the course will not be set up to be as difficult as courses typically used at county fairs or at state level events. Each student will have an opportunity to have a practice drive, or more if needed, before making their official drive. The teacher and student committee should arrange to have a couple of judges to score each student. An individual from a local tractor dealership or perhaps a local farmer would be good choices. The teacher and judges should provide close supervision of the CDE.

Conclusion

The scores from the written exercise on safety rules will be combined with the tractor driving score to determine the results of the CDE. At the next FFA meeting students would be recognized and presented their awards. If desired, recognition could be given at three standard levels such as gold, silver and bronze. Pictures taken of the students driving the tractor could constitute a bulletin board display in the classroom or in the foyer of the school. The teacher will evaluate the entire process and make notes for improvements that should be made for the next year.

Appendix B

Conducting a Local LDE in Employment Skills
Employment Skills LDE

Introduction

Before beginning the instruction on employment skills, the students will be told what lessons will be taught, about the class LDE to be held at the conclusion of the instruction, and the opportunity to advance to the chapter, region, state, and national LDE. Also, they will be told what the standard of performance to be recognized at the local FFA meeting is and will be shown the certificate that they will receive at the chapter meeting for attaining that standard. They will also be told they and their parents will receive a congratulatory letter from the teacher and chapter president. This will be taught to the class or classes where employment skills are included in the course of study.

Lessons to Be Taught

1) How does one prepare to be job ready?

The teacher will lead the class to realize that, in most cases, one doesn't just get hired for a job without a plan. The class will need to realize that in today's world of work one needs to have a well-prepared resume, attached to a well-written cover letter, to have an opportunity to be selected for an interview. The interview, in many cases, will determine whether one will be offered the position. It is essential that the interview goes well. Students will need to understand that for most of the better jobs there is competition, and they must be well-prepared to be successful.

2) How should a resume be prepared?

After instruction on what should be included in a resume, including the sharing of sample resumes, have students prepare resumes under the direction and supervision of the teacher. Instruction will include student reading, writing, and computer work. Resumes will be taken up, general and specific written suggestions will be made for improvement and returned to the students to correct and improve. After correcting, they will be taken up again and reviewed with final written suggestions before being returned. Students will then finalize their resumes. At this point the teacher will grade the resumes.

3) How should a job application cover letter be written?

After instruction on how a cover letter should be written, including showing sample cover letters, students will prepare cover letters under the direction and supervision of the teacher. Instruction will include student reading, writing, and computer work. Cover letters will be taken up, and written suggestions will be made for improvement and returned for students to correct. They will then be taken up and again reviewed with final written suggestions before being returned. Students will then finalize their cover letters. The teacher will evaluate and grade each cover letter.

4) How does one have an effective job interview?

After instruction, including showing a video of a job interview, a selected student(s) will have a brief interview with the teacher. The teacher will lead a class critique of the interview(s), then all students will be placed in groups and interviews will be conducted by school personnel and the teacher. Each student's interview will be evaluated by the interviewer and the students in their group. Following this practice at interviewing, a class interview event will be held with these interviews being scored by the students and the teacher.

Additional Methodology

For each of the four lessons, the teacher will guide the class to identify the things to consider for solving the question/problem, and then the students will read or research references and write an individual conclusion. The teacher will then guide the class making use of their research and conclusion to reach a class conclusion.

After each class conclusion is completed, the methodology described in each lesson will be implemented.

Chapter LDE

The teacher and a committee of students will be responsible for evaluating the grades on the resume, cover letter, and interviews to determine who and how many students will go on to the chapter LDE.

The chapter LDE will be judged by individuals such as Regional Manager for Southern States, a representative of Tractor Supply Company, and the personnel director of the school system.

Conclusion

All students deemed as having done an excellent job will receive a certificate of excellence at the next chapter FFA meeting. They will be called to the front and have their names read, receive their certificate, and a handshake from all the FFA officers. The first-place student will represent the chapter at the next level. A letter of congratulations will be sent to the parents whose child met the standard of excellence in the LDE.

The teacher will evaluate the entire process, strengths and weaknesses, and make notes for improvement for the next year. The chapter level LDE might be videoed, retaining the winner's video to show next year's class. Also, the teacher may keep copies of some of the better cover letters and resumes to show next year's class. The agriculture teacher may also consider involving a business teacher and/or an English teacher in helping to select the students to move from the class level to the chapter level.

Acknowledgements

Sincere gratitude is extended to the many individuals who have impacted both my philosophy of life and education. Key individuals who have made specific contributions to the 17 principles outlined in this publication include: Mr. Charles L. Eldridge, my high school agriculture teacher, Dr. Harold R. Binkley, University of Kentucky teacher educator and co-author of our book, *Handbook on Student Organizations in Vocational Education*, and Dr. Ralph E. Bender, my Ohio State doctoral committee chair. Although these great men are deceased, their teachings live on.

I also wish to express gratitude to each classmate and teacher from my early elementary years, high school and higher education. A special acknowledgment goes to my own students at Lowes High School and the University of Kentucky. I also thank Lowes High School principal, Mr. W.W. Chumbler (deceased), who provided support, encouragement, and freedom to teach when I was at the genesis of my career.

Credit also must be given to my children, Melanie Byers Stivers and Keith Byers, who provided anecdotal narrative for some of my principles. Finally, a special thank you to Dr. Wm. Jay Jackman, Executive Director, National Association of Agricultural Educators, and Ms. Alissa Smith, Chief Executive Officer, National Association of Agricultural Educators. These two former students gave birth to the idea of putting these seventeen principles to print and supported the idea as it became a reality.

Bacchante Books
Lexington, KY